Joseph
The Journey to Forgiveness

A Bible Study by
Melissa Spoelstra

A Preview Book

Abingdon Press
Nashville

JOSEPH:
THE JOURNEY TO FORGIVENESS
A Preview Book

Contents

Introduction

Do you ever find your mind replaying old tapes of wrongs done to you? Have you walked into a room, spotted someone who has hurt you in some way, and wanted to walk the other direction and hope the person didn't see you? Maybe your pain runs deep from fresh wounds, or perhaps your scars leave a daily reminder of discomfort from the past. All of us know what it's like to feel betrayed by someone we trusted. Often it's a small breach such as being overlooked, having a demeaning comment made about you in front of others, or being neglected in a time of need. Other times we've experienced lies, gossip, or harsh words that cut us to the core. Some of us have endured unspeakable pain through abuse, adultery, or abandonment.

The consequences of holding on to the hurt inflicted by others can ruin the way we view God, ourselves, and other relationships. The stakes of forgiveness are high, and when betrayal gets personal in our lives, it certainly isn't easy.

Nowhere do we see forgiveness played out more fully in Scripture than in the biblical story of Joseph in the Old Testament. No sugarcoating there. Forgiveness rises to the top in this story, but not without the messy grappling with grace that we all encounter. Through this snapshot preview of Joseph's story of trial and triumph (which I explore in depth in my Bible study by the same title, *Joseph: The Journey to Forgiveness*), we will find that God has much to teach us. Joseph's dreams, betrayers, dysfunctional family, and journey toward reconciliation will reveal truths that echo into our own personal situations. I invite you to join me on the journey to find freedom through forgiveness.

1.

Acknowledging the Pain

Genesis 37; 39

We don't have to look much farther than our own front door to find a place to practice forgiveness. Living in close proximity to others provides many opportunities to hurt one another. With pretenses down, we unveil our true selves at home. Family members see what we hide from others outside our four walls.

I've heard it said that the true test of a Christian is how he or she lives at home. Families are the people committed to love us even when our flaws are exposed. Whether through birth, adoption, or the covenant of marriage, family connections often involve our closest relationships: husband and wife, parent and child, sister and brother, grandparent and grandchild.

This was certainly true for Joseph. His father's favor and God-given dreams contributed to friction with his brothers. They were jealous and unkind to Joseph. Their negative emotions led them to plot his murder, throw him in a pit, and ultimately sell him into slavery.

The First Step

Through the account of Joseph and his brothers in Genesis 37, we find that the first step on the journey to forgiveness is acknowledging the hurt. We can never forgive without getting honest about our pain. Joseph's brothers endured some unfair neglect because of a birth order they had no control over. Whether they intended to or not, Jacob and Joseph caused pain for the brothers. And the brothers had the choice of working toward forgiveness or vengeance. Though you may not be struggling with being on the wrong end of favoritism as Joseph's brothers were, it's likely that you are carrying some pain at the expense of others.

If we stuff or ignore our pain, we can't bring it to God for healing. This can leave us with festering negativity that can lead to bitterness. God wants to help us through the hurt so that we can be free to embrace His forgiveness and extend it to others.

The psalmist reminds us of God's care for us when others have said or done hurtful things:

"You keep track of all my sorrows. / You have collected all my tears in your bottle. / You have recorded each one in your book" (Psalm 56:8).

Tell God how you feel about whatever hurt you are experiencing right now. He saw it happen. He longs to listen and talk with you about it. He has collected every tear. Acknowledge the hurt to the One who cares more than anyone else on this planet and who offers His comfort to you.

Fuel to the Fire

Have you ever felt the sting of pain in a relationship and questioned yourself about what part you might have played in contributing to the problems? I know I have. If we have played a role in creating the circumstances that have led to our injury or betrayal, are the others involved still to be held accountable for what has happened? If we have been "provoked" by another person, can we excuse our reaction? These are the kinds of practical questions that often torment us. Clarifying who and what warrants forgiveness is vital in our journey toward healing.

While Joseph reported on his brothers, wore a coat signifying his favor, and told his family of his dreams to rule over them, he is not to blame for the actions of his brothers. He did not make them commit assault and kidnapping. In the same way, people can push our buttons; but ultimately we are responsible for our actions. We have a choice of which posture we will assume when legitimate hurt comes into our lives. Which will we take?

- A victim mentality, seeing ourselves at the mercy of our pain

or

- A victor mentality, acknowledging the hurt while seeking God's help in pursuing healing

How have you struggled with these two internal postures? What helps you move from victim to victor in your heart and mind when you are struggling with pain? Even if another person fans the flames of our pain, God calls us to forgive rather than excuse ourselves to disobey His commands.

It's always our turn to do the right thing for the right reasons. Forgiveness isn't one option on a list of possible choices for followers of Jesus; it is the only way to peace and freedom.

Taming the Wild Horses

After acknowledging the hurt, we also have to recognize the negative emotions that usually follow pain. A friend of mine shared with me how she taught her daughters from a young age about their emotions. She said emotions are like wild horses who want to jump, kick, and make loud noises. In order to tame the wild horses within, we can't stuff our feelings. They will leak out one way or another. Instead, we must get honest in front of God and others about the emotions that betrayals or hurtful actions unearth in us and ask God for help.

At times we all feel negative emotions toward persons who hurt us, so what are we to do with those emotions? We have options just as Joseph's brothers had. We can:

- Dwell on it and let it fester inside.
- Take steps of vengeance against those we perceive to be the source of our pain.
- Ask God to help us heal.

Sometimes we do all of these. The tough question is, Where do we start when we want to heal but the wild horses won't stop thrashing about in our hearts and minds? Joseph's brothers chose vengeance, which led to other negative decisions such as covering up the crime with lies. But we can make a different choice. First John 3:20 says, "Even if we feel guilty, God is greater than our feelings, and he knows everything." As we will see throughout the Genesis narrative, Joseph knew that God was greater than his feelings, and he learned to tame his wild horses. I pray you'll remain open to how God wants to work in your life as we learn how Joseph was able to take his hurt and hate to God and find healing. Remember, God is greater than your feelings, and He knows everything!

The Before and the After

In *Great Expectations,* the famous novel by Charles Dickens, Miss Havisham encounters a traumatic betrayal when her fiancé leaves her jilted at the altar. She lives out the rest of her days wearing her bridal gown, with every clock in her house stopped on the moment she got word of the betrayal. The cake begins to rot on the table while Miss Havisham's dress becomes tattered and faded. She lives only to inflict her pain on those around her. She never recovers from the day the clocks stopped in her life.

Have you ever experienced a moment when your world seemed to change in an instant? Perhaps you learned of the betrayal of a friend or spouse or the death of a loved one. Maybe you expected a promotion only to leave your boss's office bewildered by the news of termination. Or perhaps you've experienced emotional, physical, or sexual abuse.

Joseph could have divided his life into the same two categories: before and after his brothers betrayed him. I can only imagine seventeen-year-old Joseph in the bottom of that pit. Was he begging his brothers to release him? Joseph went from hero to zero in a very short time. While we may never be able to make sense of the devastation that often invades our lives when we least expect it, we can find glimpses of hope in the midst of our despair just as Joseph did. His clocks didn't stop forever like Miss Havisham's. Instead, he found a road to healing even while living in captivity.

Whether you are living in the "before" or "after" of some difficult event or time in your life, take a moment to count the blessings from God that you've seen just this week. Has He provided for a financial need? Has He given you grace to deal with difficult people? Has He prospered your work? Did He bring some relief from physical pain? Like the psalmist, take this posture: "My eyes strain to see . . . / the truth of your promise fulfilled" (Psalm 119:123). God is faithful. Ask Him to give you eyes to see His favor that otherwise you might have missed through the haze of hardship.

Run for Your Life

Running is usually a mark of a coward, but sometimes God calls us to flee. When Potiphar's wife tempted Joseph daily by inviting him to sleep with her, he learned to stay out of her way. Then when she cornered him in the house and insisted she get her way, he ran! The Apostle Paul wrote, "Flee the evil desires of youth and pursue righteousness, faith, love and peace, along with those who call on the LORD out of a pure heart" (2 Timothy 2:22 NIV). God also might call us to flee a toxic relationship, a compromising job, or a spiritually abusive relationship or group. While we can't run away from every problem, there is a time when God says the best thing to do is get out of Dodge.

Take a moment to get quiet and listen to God. Where do you sense someone feeding your temptation to sin in an area that you are trying to overcome? What steps might He be calling you to take to put some distance between you and a source of continual temptation?

Staying focused on God's truth over human desire cost Joseph greatly. It led to a second betrayal, which took him from his initial captivity as a slave in Potiphar's house to a much worse imprisonment. Just as we can't sort out all the reasons for the difficult circumstances in our own lives, we don't know for sure why these bad things happened to Joseph. However, as we read on in Genesis 39, we find that even in the depths of an Egyptian prison, God showed Joseph favor. "But the LORD was with Joseph in the prison and showed him his faithful love. And the LORD made Joseph a favorite with the prison warden" (Genesis 39:21). God continues to bless us even when we feel like we can't sink any lower. He is crazy about us! Though we can't always make sense of the whys and hows of what we're enduring when others hurt us, we can rest assured that God will never leave us or forsake us.

2.

Waiting to Be Remembered

Genesis 40

As I sat in a cute little tearoom, I listened to a friend recount her story of pain. She had taught Bible studies, blogged, and led in the women's ministry at her local church. Leading, writing, and speaking energized her as she felt equipped and called of God to use her gifts to serve others. After a series of misunderstandings, a group of women's ministry leaders asked her to step down from her position of teaching.

She questioned herself, wondering how things had come to this and exactly how she was to use her God-given gifts. After some time to process and pray, she humbly asked the women's leaders for a path back into ministry. They confirmed her call and her ability as a teacher and gave her constructive feedback. However, there was no place for her to teach in women's ministry at that time. As we sat having tea several months later, she was still waiting for the path back to become clear.

Joseph knew what it was like to wait for people to remember him. He was waiting for his God-given dreams to come true with no evidence that things would change anytime soon.

Keeping the Dream Alive

During periods of waiting and isolation such as Joseph experienced, we have much time to think and process our circumstances. These are days when bitterness is knocking on our door, bidding us to nurse unforgiveness and build walls to keep others out. Joseph couldn't control his circumstances, but he could govern his own spirit. Though initially he may have flaunted his father's favoritism, he learned to work hard, honor God, and maintain integrity even during his time of captivity. Proverbs 25:28 says, "Whoever has no rule over his own spirit / Is like a city broken down, without walls" (NKJV).

Of course, Joseph was human, just as we are. He probably didn't respond to the challenges and hurts in his life with thoughts such as these:

- My brothers' betrayal is such a great opportunity for personal growth.

- It was worth it to be tempted by Potiphar's wife every day and then falsely accused when I chose to do the right thing.
- I'm so glad the cupbearer forgot me so that I can suffer longer here in prison.

I'm guessing Joseph had to work through the hurt and the hate. However, he was able to move toward healing and right responses as evidenced by his attitude of concern for the baker and cupbearer. If he had lingered in his own personal pity party, he probably would not have been able to help the two prisoners he encountered. As we see with other biblical characters, God is more concerned with Joseph's character than with his comfort.

I find that the same holds true in my life. God seems more concerned about my character than He is about my comfort. Can you relate?

In our times of waiting, God prepares us for new beginnings. Whether they are big or small, we all have realities that we can't change in life. Like Joseph, the only variable we can control is how we will choose to respond to these events and the people involved in them. Will we maintain our integrity when no one is looking? Will we choose joy even when our circumstances go from bad to worse? Will we posture ourselves for forgiveness or vengeance?

If you are in a time of waiting, ask God to soften your heart and identify any areas where you might have seeds of bitterness taking root. Ask Him to reveal areas of unforgiveness that need to be brought to light.

Forgiveness and Justice

Joseph's story brings to the surface some tough questions: Does choosing to forgive condone injustice? Are some sins unforgivable? As Joseph languishes in prison, is he giving up on justice if he forgives his brothers and Potiphar's wife? These are tough questions. The prison years in Joseph's life are critical because it is in such times of waiting and darkness where we make secret choices of the heart and mind that shape how we act and speak later.

It's important to note that Joseph acknowledged he had been mistreated and asked for help during his waiting years. Though ultimately Joseph forgave the brothers who kidnapped and sold him, he never says that what they did was okay. This distinction is of great importance.

Forgiving someone doesn't excuse or minimize the pain that the person has caused, and often consequences remain for those who have sinned against us. It is possible to forgive others and still hold them accountable for their behavior.

We can forgive others while speaking up about their actions and asking for help in seeking justice on our behalf.

I sometimes find in Christian circles that speaking up about wrongs done to us and asking for justice is equated with a lack of forgiveness. However, the two are not mutually exclusive. We can speak up and ask for help in righting the wrongs committed against us while simultaneously working through the stages of forgiveness. Whatever hurtful situation you are experiencing, look around you in your time of waiting to see if there is someone you can share your burden with, and then ask this person for help. Whether you need compassion or a specific action to be taken on your behalf, follow God's Spirit in taking steps to ask for it.

Discerning Through the Haze

As Joseph sat in his time of waiting, he had a choice about which thoughts and feelings he would dwell on and nurture. Like us, his default would be to rehearse wrongs, let bitterness grow, and allow his wounds to fester. What we naturally want to do in a relational situation is often the wrong thing.

Joseph seems to have learned to see people through God's glasses. People are a hodgepodge of love, selfishness, kindness, fear, and the list could go on. No one is perfect. Most people aren't truly evil. They are just people who make some good decisions and some pretty bad ones. The battle for truth in relationships is often fought in our own heads and hearts. We need God's Holy Spirit desperately so that He can help us see people clearly, soften our hearts, and revise our feelings to fall in line with His.

God longs to free us from the wasted hours of fanaticizing about our villain's demise. Joseph probably did a little bit of that. He was human. But he would have had to get off the mental hamster wheel of negative thoughts toward his brothers and his boss in order to bring his thoughts and feelings into line with God's grace. We can't create eyes of grace on our own. They come only as we surrender our thought life to God, moment by moment.

Perhaps for years some of us will regularly think of the person who wronged us. What will we do with these thoughts? Second Corinthians 10:5 says, "We demolish arguments and every pretension that sets itself up against the knowledge of God, and we take captive every thought to make it obedient to Christ" (NIV). Captives don't get to do what they want to do or go where they want to go. Paul tells us to put our unforgiving thoughts into a prison cell. We are the wardens of our minds. God tells us that, with the power of the Holy Spirit, we can take thoughts captive and make them obey Christ.

How Big of a Deal Is It?

As I've sat with so many women listening to their forgiveness stories, I've found that usually the ones who are willing to share are those who have gone through a significant betrayal. Each of them certainly can relate to Joseph. Others don't have big situations but must work through a multitude of little offenses. Joseph also would have experienced smaller forgiveness opportunities, perhaps from other prisoners, the warden of the jail, or the cupbearer who forgot him. How did Joseph determine how to handle the myriad of different hurts and learn to trust God with the big and small things? Like Joseph, we must ask God for wisdom to discover when our pain is from the difficulties of living in this world, our own ultra-sensitivity, or real wrongs perpetrated against us.

As we look at the things others have done to us, we also must consider the extent of the damage. Adam Hamilton uses the example of filling a backpack with our unforgiven blows that come in different sizes. In his book *Forgiveness: Finding Peace Through Letting Go*, he explains the difference between pebbles, medium-sized rocks, and big rocks.[1] Sometimes, there is no one to forgive. We may be hurting from circumstances or a perceived slight when no one maliciously set out to hurt us. Other times we make an allowance for a fault, choosing to let love cover the offense. First Peter 4:8 says, "Most important of all, continue to show deep love for each other, for love covers a multitude of sins."

Sometimes sins against us must be confronted. This is when we follow Matthew 18:15-17, first going privately to our offender and eventually involving others or the church if the situation escalates. Although we might like to just sing a song from the Disney movie *Frozen* and be free to "Let It Go," sometimes God calls us to take some steps in the releasing process. Ask Him to make clear what next steps you may need to take in your flight to freedom. If Joseph could forgive with God's help, I believe we can, too—whether our backpack is full of pebbles or boulders.

Take a few minutes to meditate on and pray this verse to your loving God, who longs to help you discern through the haze of your pain:

O Lord, listen to my cry;
give me the discerning mind you promised.
(Psalm 119:169)

The Great Forgiver

In general, would you consider yourself an easily offended person? Consider the statement that is closest to how you think others would describe you.

- Most things roll off my back, and I don't take things personally very often.
- When someone says or does something hurtful to me, I initially get pretty upset. But I try not to make assumptions about motives and give the person the benefit of the doubt.
- Often I read things into people's facial expressions, body language, and comments that I find offensive. I don't say anything to them personally, but later I discuss it with someone who is close to me.
- People walk on eggshells around me because they know I can be offended pretty easily, and I will let them know about it too!

Christ modeled perfect forgiveness for us in life and in death. In Luke 23:34 we find his response to those who beat, mocked, unjustly accused, and tortured him: "Father, forgive them, for they don't know what they are doing." Imagine taking that posture in the very moment someone is hurting you. As you process the hurt in your life right now, the key to freedom from bitterness comes as you embrace God's complete forgiveness for you. This will help color how you view even those who have done evil things that have impacted your life dramatically.

Although Joseph did not know the gospel of Christ, he knew of God's desire to rescue His people through the stories of Noah, Abraham, his grandfather Isaac, and his father Jacob. He trusted by faith in the amount of revelation that he had received. We have an even fuller understanding of God's grace and salvation. Our God sent His own Son to die on our behalf. He held nothing back to atone for our sins and erase the debt that we could never repay. He washed our sins away completely.

How does realizing God's grace toward you help you move toward forgiving those who have hurt you? By focusing on truth and gaining perspective on the offenses of others in light of the offenses God has forgiven us, we can forgive as we've been forgiven.

3.

Dreams Coming True

Genesis 41–42

Joseph spent a long time in an in-between place. Even while in prison, he held to his clear dreams of leadership and authority, which bore no resemblance to the landscape of servitude where he found himself living. Had God forgotten him? Some days it might have seemed that way as he wore shackles on his feet and an iron collar around his neck.

Joseph believed that God was working out His invisible plans even during dark days. Though he lived on the "bottom floor" of prison, somehow he trusted that there was a "second story"—an upper level where God was doing a work. Joseph couldn't understand it, but he chose to believe there was a greater plan. Warren Wiersbe writes, "Joseph had time to think and pray and to ponder the meaning of the two dreams God had sent him. He would learn that God's delays are not God's denials."[2]

Joseph's dream began to come true as he was given a new name, a new title as second in command of Egypt, and a new wife—and eventually children. As times of waiting come to an end in our lives, we find new challenges awaiting us on the other side. We must stay totally dependent on God even when things get better circumstantially.

The Second Story

When I remember that Joseph's dreams were of his brothers' sheaves of grain bowing down to his, and of him ruling over the sun and moon and eleven stars, it's a wonder to me that Joseph maintained such a high view of God even when these dreams were indefinitely delayed. If I put myself in his shoes—in prison, suffering unjustly—I might have responded to the cupbearer's and baker's dreams like this: "I wouldn't put too much stock in those dreams. I had one about ruling, and look at me now. If I were you, I would try as hard as possible to forget those nightmares."

Joseph didn't perpetuate a pity party as I sometimes have done over much less important things. He had faith that God was still going to fulfill His promises to elevate him. He knew there was a second story where God was at work. By deciding to interpret the two servants' dreams and ask the cupbearer for help, he later found that they became the linchpin that knocked down his prison walls. Joseph's small decision to discern the meaning of their dreams—both of which came to pass just as he had said—ultimately were his ticket out of prison.

Two years went by before the cupbearer remembered Joseph—two long years before his circumstances budged at all. Yet serious dream fulfillment eventually would follow this seemingly forgotten kindness to a servant.

In my own life, I often find God working in the "smalls"—those decisions when no one is looking; that risk you take because God's Holy Spirit keeps nagging you to step out in faith; a friend you invite over who later becomes a lifelong kindred spirit. Our obedience in the smalls echoes big into the future. God calls us to be faithful in all things, believing in His goodness in the midst of bad circumstances. Where is God calling you to follow Him in what seems like a small, insignificant decision?

Every choice we make today will have an impact for God's kingdom. Whether we're at work with projects to complete or at home with a laundry basket in front of us, what we decide matters. Choose God instead of the path of least resistance, and you'll be amazed when the door of your personal prison might just swing wide open in an unexpected way.

Humble and Bold

Pharaoh couldn't sleep when dreams interrupted his slumber. Has anything been keeping you up at night? When you feel overwhelmed with the need to forgive, you can learn from Joseph's example. When he was called up from the dungeon to stand before the most powerful man in the empire, Joseph humbly admitted that dream interpretation was beyond him: "'It is beyond my power to do this,' Joseph replied. 'But God can tell you what it means and set you at ease'" (Genesis 41:16). We need to stop trying to fix our own problems or those of others around us. Like Joseph, we must start by admitting that we can't do it on our own. We need God's help. The posture of humility displayed in this scene before Pharaoh's throne echoes with relevancy into so many facets of life.

God doesn't leave us in a state of helplessness when we realize we can't solve our problems on our own. He wants to provide insight and set our minds at ease. He doesn't want us to continue in sleepless agony over things we can't understand, much less change. We can say along with Joseph, "It is beyond my power to do this . . . But God . . ." Those last two words change everything. This verse does not evoke a picture of Joseph shuffling his feet and looking at the floor like a foreign prisoner. We see a bold Joseph who is sure of himself, commanding the room. His confidence is not in himself but in the God who has helped him take steps toward forgiveness in a dungeon for the last few years.

Take a minute right now and make a similar statement to God:

> God, I can't figure out_____
> _____ on my own anymore. It is
> not in my power to do it.

Coupled with Joseph's humility was his boldness. He believed his God could do anything. Finish your prayer in this way:

> God, I boldly proclaim that You have got
> this situation. Please put my mind at ease
> and show me what You are calling me to
> do next.

You might be tempted to take back what you just released to God. I have a feeling that Joseph regularly practiced surrender. It wasn't just a one-time thing. So next time sleep won't come, remember to practice the humility and boldness of

Joseph, and you just might find a new direction for the future taking shape in your life.

From Zero to Hero

Now we've reached the point in the story where the tide really begins to turn for Joseph. He will go from serving inmates and cleaning out prison cells to a place of great power and authority. I can imagine his joy at simple pleasures that had been denied him for so long. He could walk around freely, take baths, eat good food, and enjoy his wife and children. Family had been something stolen from him long ago. Now he has a family of his own.

As second in command, Joseph would have the power to get back at Potiphar, Potiphar's wife, and even the cupbearer for forgetting him for two long years. But this isn't what we read in the text. Instead we find Joseph celebrating his new blessings and working hard to oversee a divine plan to save people from famine.

As I think about my own life, I know I have been guilty of allowing one small negative thought to ruin my ability to see the many blessings around me. Can you relate? As you think about the blessings in your life (freedom, clean water, nourishing relationships, and others), can you think of something that might be hindering you from fully appreciating them? It might be a grudge against a friend or family member that just keeps spoiling your ability to enjoy life. A difficult marriage might overshadow blessings of children and friendships. Perhaps you are reading meaning into the words from a text or social media comment, and your overanalytical brain won't stop making assumptions. Whatever it may be, we can learn from Joseph's example of appreciation and productivity.

What task has God put in front of you that could shift your focus from negative thoughts to productive energy? Leviticus 19:18 (NIV) says, "Do not seek revenge or bear a grudge against anyone among your people, but love your neighbor as yourself. I am the LORD."

As you shift from dwelling on the past to focusing on this task from God, you can gain some ground toward forgiveness and the ability to more fully enjoy your blessings.

Responders and Reactors

In today's world of social media and instant communication, we need even greater restraint when faced with situations that tempt us to react. Whether we are coming face-to-face with those who have hurt us or giving an answer when an offense is brought against us, the inclination to say or do something immediately can be overwhelming. I know I am especially sensitive to this when others criticize my children. I've also witnessed some great friendships torn apart over skirmishes between children, extended family members, or mutual friends. We need time to see things clearly so that we don't act first and think later.

Can you recall a time in your life when you found yourself face-to-face with a person who had hurt you in the past? If so, what were some of the emotions you experienced? Did you react, respond, or avoid the situation?

Every human on the planet struggles to patiently respond instead of emotionally react. We find Joseph having a very emotional day in this next part of his story. In Genesis 42 we find his face-to-face encounter with his brothers.

When his brothers traveled to Egypt in search of grain, they didn't recognize Joseph. He certainly recognized them! However, he didn't reveal his identity right away. His initial reaction to them was to falsely accuse them and put them in prison for three days. During that time we saw Joseph soften his original decision and speak much more kindly and clearheaded: "On the third day Joseph said to them, 'I am a God-fearing man. If you do as I say, you will live. If you really are honest men, choose one of your brothers to remain in prison. The rest of you may go on home with grain for your starving families. But you must bring your youngest brother back to me. This will prove that you are telling the truth, and you will not die.' To this they agreed" (Genesis 42:18-20).

Joseph took three days for his rule of response. In our fast-paced world, you might not have three full days to respond; but at least try to follow the twenty-four-hour rule. Whatever it is that you want to react to—big or small—just wait. Think. Pray. Ask God for wisdom. Allow time for your emotions to settle so that you can see things more clearly. As we continue to learn from Joseph's example, may we be careful to remember his rule of response. In order to see God's bigger plan and give time for emotions to settle, we must learn to wait before taking action so that we can be responders instead of reactors.

Testing before Trusting

Have you ever encountered an "unsafe" person? Dee Brestin describes these people as alligators in her book *The Friendships of Women*. They can inflict wounds that go beyond surface scratches, leaving scars from their bites. She explains, "Alligators demonstrate a pattern of destruction. Every rose has a few thorns, but an alligator is covered with them."[3] As his brothers reappeared in

Joseph's life, he needs to determine their character. He hasn't seen them in so long, and he has changed much over the course of time while serving in Potiphar's house, enduring prison, and serving as a royal official under Pharaoh.

Now he needs to see what his brothers are really like. When he was seventeen, he didn't realize how unsafe they were until he was pleading with them from the bottom of a pit. He won't make the same mistake again. So he sets up opportunities to test them and evaluate whether he can reconcile with them and invite his wife and children into relationship with them. In the meantime, he would like to see his father and younger brother. While he tests to see if the brothers merely have thorns or continue to be alligators, it appears that he seeks God's wisdom for each step of discovery.

Can you remember a time when you have tested to evaluate whether a particular relationship fell into the rose with thorns or alligator category? How did the time of testing reveal the character of the individual?

Under pressure, our true natures are exposed. When conflict or difficulty puts our relationships to the test, we must seek God's help to determine whether our pain is simply a surface scratch or an alligator bite so that we can know what next steps to take.

4.

The Roller Coaster Ride

Genesis 43–44

Have you ever forgiven someone but not been able to reconcile with the person? Forgiveness and reconciliation are not the same thing. We are always called to forgive others through the power of God working in our lives. To forgive, we acknowledge the hurt and strong emotions that accompany the pain and then ask God to help us freely let go of the offense. The Hebrew word for forgive is *nasa*, which means "to lift up."[4] When we forgive, we lift up the pain to God and require no penance or payment from our offender. Forgiveness takes only one person and happens on the inside of a person.

Reconciliation, on the other hand, takes two people. Only after both parties have repented of any wrongdoing toward the other can they come close again in relationship. After reconciliation, the relationship may be even better than before the offense or may require new boundaries, depending on how both parties behave after they have reunited.

The process to both forgiveness and reconciliation is not clear-cut and differs from person to person. In other words, there is not one right way. Sometimes we forgive quickly and then spend a long time reconciling. Other times we struggle with forgiveness forever and then quickly reconcile. There are as many different scenarios as there are roller coaster rides.

Withholding in a Famine

As we continue Joseph's story, we find the harsh famine years greatly impacting his father and brothers' families in Canaan. The rain isn't falling, whether they like it or not.

Are you facing a situation that you have no control over right now? What famine in your life is causing you to feel dry and limited?

Jacob did not want to let his boys travel back to Egypt for more grain because he knew the Egyptian official had stated that they had to bring their youngest brother, Benjamin, back with them when they came. Jacob had lost Joseph, and he couldn't bear the possibility of losing Benjamin too. Here we find Jacob withholding out of fear. His fear led him to hold on to unrealistic expectations, blame others for situations beyond anyone's control, and feel paralyzed by grief.

Can you relate to these unhealthy tendencies as you face your own fears? Ultimately, Jacob put his trust in El Shaddai, the All-Sufficient One. Like Jacob, we too can easily forget God's great promises to be all that we need. Essentially we have the same options. We can choose bitterness, or we can grow through grief and prepare to follow God. And here's the good news: we can choose to follow God even if we trust Him only after exhausting every other option, we are still scared to release something or someone, or our faith resembles cynical resignation.

How can you focus more on God's character than your fears today? He is your All-Sufficient El Shaddai asking you to trust Him because He loves you and always has your best interests in mind. "Such love has no fear, because perfect love expels all fear. If we are afraid, it is for fear of punishment, and this shows that we have not fully experienced his perfect love" (1 John 4:18).

Buckle Up

We see the roller coaster ride reaching a high as the brothers arrive back in Egypt and find out they are invited to Joseph's house. The brothers might have thought they had missed the window to free their brother Simeon, who had remained in prison, and buy more food from this ruler in Egypt. Can you imagine their fear escalating as they wait for him in his home? Perhaps they thought, *What if he won't give us food? What if he kills us all?* After all, this ruler had been harsh to them last time, even accusing them as spies. No wonder they were reluctant to return.

I can relate. There have been times when I have been tempted to think I have reached the point of no return in relationships, believing that too much time has passed to reconnect or reconcile. Have you ever thought that it was too late to reconcile a relationship? There is no statute of limitations on reconciliation. Reconciliation itself takes time, and it is never too late to make it right. It may seem impossible, but we know that nothing is impossible with our God: "Jesus looked at them intently and said, 'Humanly speaking, it is impossible. But with God everything is possible'" (Matthew 19:26).

Though good things are happening circumstantially for the brothers, there is still a missing piece—authenticity. While they eat and celebrate together, there is a big elephant in the room that hasn't been addressed. Not only is Joseph's identity still hidden, but also the brothers have not repented. Repentance must precede reconciliation. Let's consider two important cautions we learn from this scene. First, we must be careful not to measure success in relationships by a lack of conflict or difficulty. Second, we must not confuse counterfeit happiness with the lasting joy of reconciliation.

Once we move beyond our paralyzing grief and board the ride toward reconciliation, we find ourselves enjoying the climb; but we must not let the roller coaster ride of reconciliation end superficially. God calls us to go deep in working toward authenticity in reconciling relationships.

Whiplash from the Ups and Downs

The concepts of grace and forgiveness are unnatural to live out. We can easily talk about them and agree they are God's way, but when it comes to actually looking at our betrayer with love, it's no easy ride. I have wished my mind could be free of negative thoughts that continue to recur about individuals who have caused me pain. When we don't care about people, it doesn't hurt so much. In contrast, when we have trusted others with our hearts, secrets, and love, the pain of rejection and betrayal isn't easily wished away.

Joseph's pain certainly wasn't a surface wound. He was even thinking of his brothers' betrayal when he named his children. His journey toward forgiveness and reconciliation was a roller coaster of ups and downs.

My downs on the roller coaster often revolve around rehearsing offenses in my mind and justifying myself, which sometimes leads me to review things the person has said or done in the past with a new judgmental bent. Some of the ups for me include focusing on God's grace toward me, praying for those who have hurt or offended me, and memorizing Scripture. One of the most helpful things when we are navigating the ups and downs of forgiveness and reconciliation is to set our minds on truth: "And now, dear brothers and sisters, one final thing. Fix your thoughts on what is true, and honorable, and right, and pure, and lovely, and admirable. Think about things that are excellent and worthy of praise" (Philippians 4:8).

The gospel truths of God's grace are a perfect place to set our minds when we are struggling with the roller coaster of thoughts and emotions related to those who have hurt us. As we study, meditate, and memorize God's Word, we find help in navigating the highs and lows of difficult relationships.

Making an Appeal

As we see the brothers being stopped outside the city, accused of stealing, and taken back to face

Joseph, we realize that Joseph likewise has been struggling through his human emotions on the road to grace and forgiveness. Joseph hid a silver cup in Benjamin's bag, which could have resulted from his struggle to show grace, but it also shows an element of wisdom related to testing.

Joseph wants to see if his brothers have changed. They so easily sold him (Dad's favorite) to get rid of him. Now they have a golden opportunity to get rid of Jacob's now-favored son, Benjamin. However, the brothers' actions reveal that two decades have changed them. Judah gives a speech in which he stands up for Benjamin, offering us a lesson in making an appeal. And whether we realize it or not, we all make appeals in our relationships, especially with those who are closest to us.

Consider these four principles of an appeal we learn from Judah's speech:

1. *Choose the right posture.* Judah speaks respectfully. He uses a tone and language that convey humility.
2. *Give the history and background information.* Before he makes his request, Judah spends the majority of his words helping the other party fully understand the complexity of the situation.
3. *Be solution oriented.* Judah proposes a sacrificial possibility to address the issue: he offers himself in Benjamin's place, playing

the role of redeemer. It's easy to point out a
problem, but finding a plausible alternative
with personal investment gives an appeal
even greater credibility.

4. *Help the person understand the consequences
   of his or her decision.* Judah points out
   that taking Benjamin will have grave
   ramifications for his father.

Is there a situation in which you feel an injustice
has been done that you would like to address? If so,
how can you apply one or more of these principles
from Judah's speech in your situation?

Getting Off the Ride

God pursues us relentlessly. He devises ways to
bring us back when we have gone astray:

> All of us must die eventually. Our lives are like
> water spilled out on the ground, which cannot be
> gathered up again. But God does not just sweep
> life away; instead, he devises ways to bring us
> back when we have been separated from him.
>
> (2 Samuel 14:14)

As you think about your walk with Christ, what
are some ways He has pursued you?

God desires a close relationship with us—His
people. He didn't even spare His own Son to

bridge the gap of sin. He asks only that we accept His offer of restitution for the sin that separates us from Him: "But to all who believed him and accepted him, he gave the right to become children of God" (John 1:12).

Forgiveness is a nonnegotiable for all Christ-followers. You might say that we are called to be professional forgivers. God modeled this for us by sending His own Son to die in our place. C. S. Lewis wrote, "To be a Christian means to forgive the inexcusable, because God forgave the inexcusable in you."[5] God calls us to forgive but doesn't leave us without His power to do it. Like a glove that moves only with a living hand inside, God's Spirit moves our forgiveness fingers as we yield to Him. The process of reconciliation, however, isn't fully dependent on our choice or actions. As we've seen, it takes at least two to reconcile. This is what distinguishes reconciliation from forgiveness. They are sisters but not twins.

> If it is possible, as far as it depends on you, live at peace with everyone. (Romans 12:18 NIV)

How does a better understanding of reconciliation and forgiveness bring clarity to your relationships?

5.

Grace and Boundaries

Personal Responsibility

To go from the point of pain to the place of extending grace toward those who wound us is truly a supernatural act that takes testing, time, and truth. We've come to a climax in the Genesis narrative with a big reveal on Joseph's part. Joseph has tested the men who had thrown him into a pit and sold him into slavery two decades earlier, and now he finds it safe to stop the charade and take off his Egyptian mask.

Joseph could stand it no longer. There were many people in the room, and he said to his attendants, "'Out, all of you!' So he was alone with his brothers when he told them who he was. Then he broke down and wept. He wept so loudly the Egyptians could hear him, and word of it quickly carried to Pharaoh's palace" (Genesis 45:1-2).

I can think of times when I have wanted to get words out but tears choked me so that it took several minutes before I could utter an explanation. It's good to be reminded that we aren't the only ones who struggle to hold it together emotionally, right?

Let's look at what we learn from Joseph's encounters with his brothers in chapters 45 and 46.

Come Closer

I can only imagine the mixture of disbelief, concern for their lives, clarity about past interactions, guilt, and many other things that could have been rolling around in the brothers' heads after Joseph revealed himself. They can't even wrap their minds around the fact that not only is their brother alive, but also his dreams of having authority over them have been realized. While they are reeling in shock, Joseph speaks again. His words provide a great model for us in the reconciling conversations we have with those who have hurt us, identifying four important concepts.

1. *Request any needed affirmations.* Doubt and worry can cause us to feel insecure throughout the reconciliation process, so we need to be willing to boldly ask for reaffirmation even if we've already been told once that things are okay.

2. *Communicate "come closer."* Remember that Joseph tested the waters first, before communicating "come closer" to his brothers. We don't invite alligators to come close. But once we have patiently, slowly, and carefully tested our offender, we need to follow Joseph's example and use words and body language that communicate the message, "Come closer."

3. *Acknowledge the truth.* Though Joseph says, "Come closer," he also states the truth of the matter: "I am Joseph, your brother, whom you sold into slavery in Egypt" (Genesis 45:4). He is not only clarifying his identity but also communicating that, from here on out, the fictitious story they have been sticking to for a long time must be replaced with truth.

4. *Focus on God.* Immediately after speaking the truth, Joseph follows it with these words: "But don't be upset, and don't be angry with yourselves for selling me to this place" (Genesis 45:5). There is no penitence necessary; it is already forgiven. Joseph doesn't play the victim card. Instead he chooses to view the barbaric

treatment he endured as something God
is using as a lifesaver for many.

How can you implement some of these principles from Joseph's declarations in your own
relationships right now?

Talking Freely

When was the last time you went a day without
food? In the same way, receiving and extending
forgiveness isn't a one-time thing. It's daily.

Give us today the food we need,
and forgive us our sins,
as we have forgiven those who sin against us.

(Matthew 6:11-12)

Forgiveness lives at the center of the gospel of
Christ. While we sometimes focus on our daily
need for it, we often forget the daily practice of
extending it. Though Joseph took his time in
revealing himself to his brothers, now that he has
done it, he is anxious to enact plans so that he
may see his beloved father. One of the blessings
of forgiving and reconciling with others is that
it can open the door to relationships that sin had
nailed shut—not only those immediately involved
but also those of mutual friends, extended family
members, and acquaintances. Whether it's a

physical or emotional barrier keeping the door shut, reconciliation can knock the rusted hinges off a door that has been impassable for decades.

Have you ever found that reconciling with someone has positively impacted other mutual relationships? How did this bring a blessing in your life?

We learn from Genesis 45:15 that "they began talking freely with him." Once again we see that Joseph doesn't shame, punish, or even make passive-aggressive references to his brothers. But we also can note some things that his brothers do not do. Here we do not find any excuses, interruptions, explanations, or corrections of details.

Though moments earlier the brothers were so shocked that they didn't respond at all, now they are talking freely—and without offering excuses or explanations. We find a different interaction here than in their previous exchanges with Joseph in Egypt or those of the early years. Talking freely is one of the many benefits of restored relationships.

Unleashing Grace

Joseph had been stripped of his robe, but after reconciling with his brothers, he provided them with clothes. While the brothers took twenty pieces of silver for their evil deed of selling their brother, Joseph generously gave Benjamin fifteen times that amount. Even Joseph's previous act of slipping money into his brothers' bags can be viewed in a positive light. Whether that was pure generosity or a way to test them in order to establish trust, we see him using shekels with good intentions. Joseph went beyond forgiving to actually blessing.

In First Peter we find these words:

> Don't repay evil for evil. Don't retaliate with insults when people insult you. Instead, pay them back with a blessing. That is what God has called you to do, and he will grant you his blessing.
>
> (1 Peter 3:9)

When we want to choose forgiveness but struggle against our feelings, we can set out to intentionally bless our offender. Instead of letting our thoughts and feelings run wild, we can turn our focus to pursuing creative ways to give a blessing.

Perhaps there is someone you have been struggling to forgive—someone who is a "relational enemy" right now. You want to move on, but you find the hurt this person has caused creeping into your daily thoughts. Jesus said, "But to you who are willing to listen, I say, love your enemies! Do good to those who hate you. Bless those who curse you. Pray for those who hurt you" (Luke 6:27-28). Are we willing to listen? What could we do to bless those who have hurt us?

Boundary Lines

As Joseph unleashed grace onto his brothers, he had a healthy sense of boundaries. Boundaries can be a difficult part of our messy forgiveness stories. After reconciling, we often struggle to find a "new normal" in an old relationship. We have seen God work through our confessions, repentance, and reunion, bringing healing where once there was hurt. Now the questions become, Where do we go from here? How can we interact in a healthy way without falling into old, destructive patterns?

Forgiveness plus grace is not a recipe for naivety. Joseph knows what his brothers are like. Reconciliation doesn't mean Joseph never advises, warns, or instructs his brothers. He actually sets a limit on how they are to treat one another by telling them not to fight on their journey back home to retrieve their families and father.

Sometimes God calls us away from difficult relationships, and other times He asks us to stay engaged and fight to make it better. With a clear boundary in place, we don't feel responsible for managing the life and emotions of others; instead, we are able to seek God for His direction in tending our own spiritual yards. We are always called to forgive those who trespass against us, but that doesn't mean we can't put up a fence so that the access to do it again is limited.

What boundaries has God asked you to put in place for emotional or physical health in a complicated relationship?

Joseph had his brothers settle in Goshen, but he didn't move there as well. He had them close, but not in his backyard. We desperately need the help of God's Spirit coupled with wisdom from His Word to know how to navigate a new normal in a reconciled relationship.

- How much of our secrets will we reveal?
- What amount of time and emotional energy will we invest?
- We may let someone into our lives, but should we let her or him into our soul?
- Are there some lines we need to draw regarding what we won't do or allow?

God will help you, lead you, and wrestle with you through the speed bumps in your relationships. Both through His Word and through His Spirit, He will reveal wisdom about boundaries in your relationships.

Moving On

Imagine Jacob's shock upon learning from his sons that Joseph is still alive! Jacob prepares to make a major move at the end of his life, but he takes the time before a significant life transition to ask for God's help and blessing.

As we enter into new phases of life such as becoming a mother, parenting teens, starting a new job, or moving to a new community, we can learn from Jacob's example the importance of taking some time out from the craziness that usually surrounds these transitions to focus on God. When we find ourselves at a crossroads, it is wise and appropriate to stop and worship God as Jacob did, reflecting on God's provision and grace and seeking His guidance.

For Jacob, who lived under the Old Testament law and worshiped God through the system of animal sacrifices (which was a shadow pointing to Jesus; see Hebrews 10:1-19), this was no quick or unplanned act. Offering a sacrifice…

- was intentional.
- took preparation and time.
- required resources or cost.

As I've reflected on Jacob's dedication, I've thought about how we could be more intentional about worshiping God during some of the crossroads moments and big moves in our own lives. The list of ways we could dedicate new phases of life to the Lord is endless, but here are just a few ideas:

- Take a day to fast, focusing on God and listening to Him (the fast could be from food, social media, or something else).
- Have a family prayer over a new home, dedicating it to God.
- Pray together as a family in the car as you prepare for a long road trip.
- Choose a book or section of the Bible to read and study during a transition in life (e.g., illness: the Book of Job; moving: Abraham's story; wedding: Song of Solomon).

What other ideas can you add to the list? If you are going through a transition right now, what is a practical way you can dedicate this new phase to God or keep your focus on Christ?

The writer of Hebrews recalls these words in the New Testament: "For God has said, / 'I will never fail you. / I will never abandon you'" (Hebrews 13:5b). God promises never to leave us. Life is a journey full of risks, fears, and what ifs, but we are never alone. He moves with us no matter where or when we go!

6.

Moving Forward

Genesis 47–50

Have you ever become weary of continually having to forgive and reconcile in a relationship? What has helped you persevere?

God calls us to stay the course and follow Him even when people never change. Joseph introduced his family to Pharaoh and cared for them. In the last few chapters of Genesis we find family blessings and changes as Joseph continues to extend love and grace.

Pilgrims

None of our pilgrimages is exactly like another's. The danger comes when we get stuck where we are and fail to see the larger picture of where we are headed. We easily forget that the road we tread right now is temporary. Our true citizenship is in heaven. We are just visitors on a journey on this planet:

> All these people died still believing what God had promised them. They did not receive what was promised, but they saw it all from a distance and welcomed it. They agreed that they were foreigners and nomads here on earth. (Hebrew 11:13)

We are foreigners and nomads here, but God has a purpose in our pilgrimage. When we realize this earth is not all there is, it affects the way we view life. As we recognize that each one of us is on a journey, it gives us compassion for our fellow sojourners. They are "in process" just as we are. I have wasted time and mental energy on resentment over past hurts, which has spoiled my ability to enjoy the present journey alongside others. I miss the blessings of today when I am stuck in resentment for things that happened yesterday. We are to walk our roads together, especially in the community of believers and in our families. If Joseph could forgive, is there anything too big to be reconciled in your life? Is there a person or situation that you need to release to God again today?

> Hear my prayer, O LORD!
>   Listen to my cries for help!
>   Don't ignore my tears.

For I am your guest—
> a traveler passing through,
> as my ancestors were before me.
>
> (Psalm 39:12)

Not What I Expected

Have you ever thought God would work in a certain way based on your own experience or the way you had seen Him work in the past? Then you were perplexed when He did something completely unexpected. Joseph got frustrated when his father, Jacob, switched his hands and gave the greater blessing to Joseph's younger son.

I probably would have struggled just as Joseph did. Considering what we see of Joseph through the Genesis narrative, my guess is that he was "type A" just like me. No matter what the test, I come out with the words systematic or detailed on my profile. I like things that make sense, go in order, and fit neatly into flow charts. For Joseph to manage Potiphar's house, give oversight in the jail, and plan and execute the food program in Egypt, he had to be an organized list maker. (I don't know about you, but I love that about him.)

Yet what seems most logical to us isn't always God's plan. Boy, have I found that to be true in my life. I have seen God work most mightily in the hardest of times that I never would have chosen. Joseph knew about receiving insight from God. Remember that Pharaoh asked Joseph to interpret his dream and Joseph said, "It is beyond my power to do this" (Genesis 41:16). He looked to God when coming out of the dungeon, but he favored tradition and logic when it came to his father blessing his boys. Like Joseph, sometimes we can struggle to trust God when He works outside of our logic box. Although He is a God of order, it is His order, not ours. His ways are perfect, but they don't always seem that way from our point of view:

> For just as the heavens are higher than the earth,
> so my ways are higher than your ways
> and my thoughts higher than your thoughts.
> (Isaiah 55:9)

His ways and thoughts transcend ours. We can't see the complete picture. If we could, we would make the same decision God would make. Forgiveness certainly lives outside the logic box. God switches His hands and opens them up, offering mercy in one and grace in the other instead of the judgment we deserve. Because of that, we too can open up our hands and offer mercy for those who have hurt us.

How can you trust God with something that doesn't seem to make sense in your world right now?

Legacy

Jacob blessed his sons with appropriate messages. Here are two takeaways we find regarding legacy in Genesis.

1. *We always have an opportunity to change direction.* Judah started out on the wrong road but eventually got back on the right path of yielding to God. If you have been walking in bitterness, resentment, or unforgiveness, you don't have to stay on that path. As you think about a time that you nursed those feelings and made choices contrary to God's clear commands, how did that work out for you? We will never find peace by pursuing our own path over God's instructions.

2. *Don't waste your suffering.* Joseph and Simeon both served unjust sentences in prison. Joseph learned through his sufferings, but Simeon did not. Living in an unfair world, we all have unique struggles. Many of them come at the hands of other

people. The posture we take toward our suffering and our offenders will greatly affect the amount of character produced in our lives.

How can you grow through your trials and mistakes, learning to love your enemies so that you can fail forward? We don't want to waste a single tear or heartache. Wasting our sufferings by staying hard-hearted and unteachable impacts the legacy we leave.

You are leaving a legacy. Is it one of forgiveness and attempted reconciliation, or is it one of hardness, bitterness, and pride? Obedience will bring blessing.

For Your Good

Forgiveness takes our initiative and faith, but comes only through the great Forgiver. By believing that God had a sovereign plan, Joseph learned to let go of the why and get to the what in his life. He never could have understood why

- God gave him dreams.
- His brothers sold him.
- Potiphar promoted him and then his wife unjustly accused him.
- He languished in prison for years.

Later he could put the pieces together and see God's hand.

We've seen Joseph wrestle with grace and test the boundaries of trust. He didn't get stuck on his journey, though. He moved forward until he got to the point where he fully embraced and continually practiced forgiveness toward his offenders. He also pursued reconciliation with boundaries to find a new normal in his relationships with his brothers.

I often struggle to let go of the *why*. I want to know immediately the purpose of my pain instead of setting my eyes on how I can learn and grow through the journey. How about you? Which one of these thoughts matches your circumstances best right now?

- I'm not struggling to figure out the *why* in anything in my life right now.
- I occasionally wonder why things are happening but not very often.
- Almost every day I contemplate *why* this particular situation is happening in my life. I want to release it and trust God, but I'm struggling.

As a human being, Joseph probably wondered why things were happening in his life. However, he learned to trust God and move forward through the good and bad times. He ultimately realized that God had a sovereign hand in all of it. He said to his brothers in Genesis 50:20, "You intended to harm me, but God intended it all for good. He brought me to this position so I could save the lives of many people." As we reconcile the conflict between how we feel and the truth of what God says, I pray God's voice will win out in your heart and mind. He wants to take all the things going on in your life right now and use them as the ingredients to make something amazing with your life.

Staying the Course

Joseph spends his last words reminding the brothers of God's truth and encouraging them to keep believing. God faithfully uses people, His Word, and all sorts of methods to remind us that He can be trusted. Today, remember that although His timing may not be yours, God will keep every promise He has made to you. The exodus from Egypt would not begin for three more centuries after Joseph's death, but God did bring His people home.

Joseph follows his father's example of wanting his eventual resting place to be the land of Canaan. However, he does not ask his brothers to take his body back right away and mourn for him as they did for Jacob. Instead, he wants his coffin to serve as a memorial to the future fulfillment of God's promise. He refers to his body as bones, knowing that the return to Canaan will not be immediate.

> It was by faith that Joseph, when he was about to die, said confidently that the people of Israel would leave Egypt. He even commanded them to take his bones with them when they left. (Hebrews 11:22)

Even in death, Joseph wants to remind others to trust God.

As we come to the end of Joseph's story, we press on in our pursuit of forgiveness. Let us ask for Joseph's perspective to trust God's sovereign plan through the daily ups and downs of life. May we ask for forgiveness like daily food—like the very breaths we breathe.

Notes

1. Adam Hamilton, *Forgiveness: Finding Peace Through Letting Go* (Nashville: Abingdon Press, 2012), 14.
2. Warren W. Wiersbe, *Be Authentic: Exhibiting Real Faith in the Real World: OT Commentary, Genesis 25–50* (Colorado Springs: David C. Cook, 1997), 111.
3. Dee Brestin, *Friendships of Women: The Beauty and Power of God's Plan for Us* (Colorado Springs: David C. Cook, 2008), 183.
4. http://www.biblestudytools.com/lexicons/hebrew/nas/nasa.html.
5. C. S. Lewis, *The Weight of Glory* (New York: HarperCollins, 2001), 182.

If you liked this book, you'll love the Bible study.

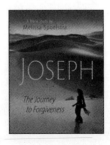

For more information about the study and
Joseph Leader Kit (ISBN 978-1-4267-8914-4), visit
AbingdonWomen.com or your favorite Christian retailer.